BART SIMPSON™
MASTER of DISASTER

TITAN BOOKS

BART SIMPSON MASTER OF DISASTER

Bart Simpson Comics # 63, 64, 65, 66, and 67

Copyright © 2016 by
Bongo Entertainment, Inc. All rights reserved.

Published in the UK by Titan Books, a division of Titan Publishing Group Ltd.,
144 Southwark St., London SE1 0UP, under licence from Bongo Entertainment, Inc.

FIRST EDITION: APRIL 2016

ISBN 9781785652547

2 4 6 8 10 9 7 5 3 1

Publisher: Matt Groening
Creative Director: Nathan Kane
Managing Editor: Terry Delegeane
Director of Operations: Robert Zaugh
Art Director: Jason Ho
Art Director Special Projects: Serban Cristescu
Assistant Art Director: Mike Rote
Production Manager: Christopher Ungar
Assistant Editor: Karen Bates
Production: Art Villanueva
Administration: Ruth Waytz
Legal Guardian: Susan A. Grode

Printed by TC Transcontinental, Beauceville, QC, Canada. 01/30/2016

MODEL BEHAVIOR

"COMIC BOOKS & BASEBALL CARDS"

OH, **MAN!** AFTER ALL THIS TIME I'VE **FINALLY** GOT MY HOT AND SWEATY HANDS ON THE RADIOACTIVE MAN RAD ROCKET RACER MODEL KIT!

DON'T FORGET **OUR** HOT AND SWEATY HANDS, BART! WE **ALL** PUT IN THE MONEY TO BUY IT!

WELL, EXCEPT **YOU**.

DON'T WORRY, I'LL PAY YOU GUYS BACK. BESIDES, IT WAS MY IDEA TO GO IN THIRDSIES ON THE MODEL. THAT'S A CONTRIBUTION, RIGHT?

EXCUSE ME? "**THIRDSIES**"? THAT'S NOT A WORD!

UH, I GUESS SO...

OH, **YEAH**? THAT'S WHAT THEY SAID ABOUT **HALFSIES**, MARTIN! **NOW** LOOK AT IT! YOU CAN GOOGLE IT AND EVERYTHING!

IT'S NOT ALLOWED IN SCRABBLE--

C'MON, GUYS, NO FIGHTING! REMEMBER THE LAST TIME WE WENT IN, UH, THIRDSIES ON SOMETHING?

TH-TH-THAT C-COMIC...THE S-STORM... M-MOMMY!

DON'T WORRY, MAN. THAT WAS THEN, AND THIS IS TOTALLY NOW. AND THE FASTER WE BUILD THIS SUCKER UP THE FASTER WE CAN ALL SHARE IT!

EVAN DORKIN
ART & STORY

SARAH DYER
COLORS

KAREN BATES
LETTERS

BILL MORRISON
EDITOR

AND SO...

OKAY, GUYS, LET'S GET THIS PARTY STARTED! TOSS ME SOME OF THOSE EXHAUST PIECES, MILHOUSE!

HOLD ON, BART, WE CAN'T JUST START BUILDING!

HUH? WHY THE HELL NOT?

ACCORDING TO THE INSTRUCTIONS WE HAVE TO CAREFULLY SEPARATE ALL THE PARTS, THEN PREWASH AND PREFIT THEM!

PFFFT! THAT'S CRAZY TALK! WHO LOOKS AT INSTRUCTIONS? YOU THINK *RADIOACTIVE MAN* READS INSTRUCTIONS?

HE HAS A POINT THERE. RADIOACTIVE MAN LAUGHS AT INSTRUCTIONS.

B-B-B-BUT...

LOOK, DUDES, MODELS PRACTICALLY BUILD THEMSELVES. YOU JUST LOOK AT THE PARTS AND YOU FIT 'EM TOGETHER.

YOU DON'T EVEN NEED ALL OF THEM! LIKE, WHO NEEDS THE ENGINE? YOU CAN'T EVEN SEE IT UNDER THE HOOD!

BUT, BART, YOU CAN'T JUST LEAVE OUT PARTS! THAT GOES AGAINST THE MODEL HOBBYISTS' CREDO.

OH, *RELAX!* WHO'LL KNOW THE DIFFERENCE, ANYWAY?

WE WILL!

IT'S PATENTLY OBVIOUS YOUR KIT-BUILDING SKILLS ARE LACKING, BART. I THINK YOU SHOULD LET US OVER-SEE THIS PROJECT!

BESIDES, WE PAID FOR IT!

OH, SO *THAT'S* HOW IT IS!

YEAH! SO HAND OVER THOSE PARTS, BART!

?

GUYS, STOP! NONE OF US CAN BUILD THE MODEL!

HUH?

WHATCHOO TALKIN' 'BOUT, MARTIN?

WE FORGOT TO BUY MODEL GLUE. SEE? IT SAYS, "GLUE NOT INCLUDED."

YOU NEED GLUE TO BUILD THIS MODEL KIT! G-L-U-E! NO GLUE NO FUN FOR YOU!

OH, *MAN*. I THOUGHT IT WAS A SNAP-TOGETHER KIT.

ME, TOO. I NEVER CHECKED. I WAS TOO BUSY LIVING IN THE MOMENT.

WHY DON'T YOU TRY *DYING* IN THE MOMENT, GENIUS?

WHERE YOU GOIN', BART?

GARAGE. HOMER'S GOTTA HAVE SOMETHIN' GLUEY WE CAN USE. HE'S GOT ALL SORTS OF STUFF IN THERE.

WHOA...IT'S LIKE A MUSEUM... DEDICATED TO THE WONDERS OF LATE-NIGHT TELEVISION MARKETING AND FAILED HOME REPAIR.

YEAH, DUDE. WHATEVER. *AHA!*

SUPER CRAZY GORILLA GLUE! "SO STRONG, EVEN *MACGYVER'S* AFRAID TO USE IT!"

IT MUST BE OLD. LIKE, MACGYVER OLD.

HMMM, I HOPE THE ADHESIVE HASN'T DRIED UP.

WARNING! DO NOT USE!

FAMILY SIZE

STICKAMOO

RELAX, BABY EINSTEIN. IT'S GOT A LIFETIME GUARANTEE! "STAYS SUPER CRAZY GORILLA STRONG, SUPER CRAZY-GORILLA-LONG!"

FAMILY SIZE

SUPER CRAZY GORILLA GLUE

"SO STRONG EVEN MacGYVER'S AFRAID TO USE IT!" — GLUEY LOUIE IT STICKS!

SO. NOW WE CAN GET BACK TO BUILDING *OUR* MODEL...RIGHT, GUYS?

FAMILY SIZE

SUPER CR GORILLA G

"SO STR EVE MacGY AF US

BART?

BART, CAN YOU HEAR ME?

OH, HOMER, HE'S *AWAKE!* *THANK GOODNESS!*

WHY'D YOU USE UP MY MONKEY GLUE, BART? DON'T YOU KNOW YOU CAN'T GET THAT JUNK ANY- MORE SINCE THEY RECALLED IT?

HOMER!

WH—WHERE AM I?

SMILE! YOU'RE ALIVE

YOU'RE IN THE HOSPITAL, BART. YOU TOOK A NASTY TUMBLE, BUT WE FIXED YOU UP JUST FINE. WE ALSO GOT YOU AND YOUR FRIENDS OUT OF A VERY *"STICKY SITUATION."* AH HEE HEE HEE!

OH WELL, AT LEAST I'M FREE FROM THOSE LOSERS--

HEY! WHO'RE YOU CALLING A LOSER?

AYE, CARUMBA! THE GLUESOME TWOSOME! WHAT GOES ON HERE?

WELL, WITH THE HOSPITAL FULL UP AFTER YOUR LITTLE JOYRIDE, WE HAD NO CHOICE BUT TO PUT YOU ALL IN THE SAME BED.

SMILE! YOU'RE ALIVE!

SO IT LOOKS LIKE YOU BOYS ARE *STUCK* WITH ONE ANOTHER FOR A FEW MORE DAYS. AH HEE HEE HEE!

HEY, I GET IT! *"STUCK"!* HA HA!

I AM IN HELL.

ME, TOO.

THIRDSIES ON THAT...

SMI YOU ALI

THE_END

THE INVINCIBLE PRINCIPAL

I AM...HOW YOU SAY?...ZE MASTER OF ZE ART, NO?

WAIT 'TIL EVERYONE GETS TO SCHOOL TOMORROW MORNING!

bart rocks

THE NEXT MORNING...

AND NOW, MY FAVORITE PART... THE *REACTION* TO MY MASTERPIECE. AFTER ALL, EVERY ARTIST LOVES HIS CRITICS.

WHA-*HUH*?!

DAVID SEIDMAN
SCRIPT

JAMES LLOYD
PENCILS

MIKE ROTE
INKS

NATHAN HAMILL
COLORS

KAREN BATES
LETTERS

BILL MORRISON
EDITOR

HA! HA! HA! HA! HA! HA!

imparting knowledge rocks

Thank your teacher!

BUT I DIDN'T DO-- I MEAN... I DID SOME OF IT, BUT--

TEE HEE!

HEE HEE!

imparting knowledge rocks thank your teacher!

BUT WHAT, BART?

COME TO MY OFFICE.

LOOK, SEYMOUR, IF YOU THINK I WROTE THAT "THANK YOUR TEACHER" HOOEY...

I KNOW YOU DIDN'T, BART.

BECAUSE I WROTE IT!

WHAT? TAG YOUR OWN SCHOOL? ARE YOU SNIFFING LIBRARY PASTE?

JUST A LITTLE.

BART, I'VE PUNISHED YOUR GRAFFITI WITH DETENTION, SUSPENSION, AND EVERYTHING ELSE...BUT NOTHING'S WORKED.

AND THEN AN IDEA STRUCK ME...

...IF YOU DEFACE MY SCHOOL, *I'LL* DEFACE YOUR DEFACING!

YOU MAY AS WELL PUT YOUR SPRAY-PAINT CANS *AWAY!*

OH, YEAH?

LET EVERY EMPTY WALL BEWARE...

...BART SIMPSON SHALL PAINT *AGAIN!*

HMM... WHY DO I GET THE FEELING MY PLAN MAY NOT BE WORKING YET?

OVER THE NEXT FEW DAYS, BART SIMPSON *DOES* PAINT AGAIN...

HEH HEH HEH...

be rude

HA! HA! HA! HA! HA! HA! HA!

be a good student!

AND AGAIN...

SKINNER CAN'T READ

HA! HA! HA! HA!

RUSKIN&NERUDA CAN'T BE READ WITHOUT BEING ADORED

SLAP!

AND AGAIN...

YOU CAN'T STOP ME. BART

YOU CAN'T STOP LOVE
i ♥ edna Krabappel
~ BART xo

BART, I DIDN'T KNOW YOU CARED.

SO NICE OF YOU TO **SPRAY** THAT YOU LOVE ME.

AARGH!

UNTIL...

1972 IS FAMOUS FOR THE **WATERGATE** BREAK-IN, THE REELECTION OF RICHARD **NIXON** AND MOST IMPORTANT OF ALL, BURT REYNOLDS' APPEARANCE IN "COSMOPOLITAN" AS THE FIRST MALE CENTERFOLD.
IN '73, BURT PLAYED GATOR MCKLUSKY IN "WHITE LIGHTNING," AND...

I'VE **GOT** TO KEEP SKINNER FROM CHANGING MY WORK! MAYBE IF I DO IT AT A TIME WHEN THE KIDS'LL SEE IT BEFORE **HE** DOES...

RIIIING!

YAAAYY!

LUNCHTIME, CHILDREN!

LUNCHTIME? THAT'S **PERFECT!**

THE END

MAGGIE'S CRIB

by ARAGONÉS

SERGIO ARAGONÉS
STORY & ART

ART VILLANUEVA
COLORS

BILL MORRISON
EDITOR

CURSE OF THE MOLEMAN

ATTENTION, CHILDREN. AS MANY OF YOU KNOW, TODAY IS THE FIRST DAY OF **SPRINGFIELD HISTORY MONTH**, A TIME WHEN WE SALUTE THE MANY FINE ACCOMPLISHMENTS OF OUR CITY AND ITS CITIZENS.

CHRIS YAMBAR SCRIPT	NINA MATSUMOTO PENCILS	MIKE ROTE INKS	NATHAN HAMILL COLORS	KAREN BATES LETTERS	BILL MORRISON EDITOR

LIKE OVEREATING AND WATCHING THE BOOB TUBE?

HOW ABOUT OUR NEVERENDING TIRE FIRE?

HOW ABOUT BLINKY, THE THREE-EYED FISH?!

AHEM! ALL VALID OBSERVATIONS. HOWEVER, THIS YEAR WE PLAN TO SHOWCASE THE EFFORTS OF OUR FINEST CITIZENS, THE PRECIOUS **CHILDREN** OF SPRINGFIELD...

HUH?!?

MATT GROENING

...WHO WILL GIVE REPORTS ABOUT MEMBERS OF OUR ADULT POPULATION. THESE PRESENTATIONS WILL BE GIVEN IN THEIR CLASSROOMS STARTING NEXT WEEK.

I THINK I'M GOING TO HURL!

YAY!

HOW EXCITING.

NOW I *KNOW* I'M GOING TO HURL!

AND THE BEST PART ABOUT THESE REPORTS IS THAT THEY WILL ACCOUNT FOR *HALF* OF YOUR FINAL GRADE.

I CAN'T WAIT TO GET STARTED!

OHHH! IS IT POSSIBLE FOR THIS DAY TO GET ANY WORSE?

AND THE VERY FIRST REPORT WILL BE GIVEN BY OUR VERY OWN *BART SIMPSON*.

I THINK MY HEAD'S ABOUT TO EXPLODE.

HAW HAW!

...FOLLOWED BY NELSON MUNTZ. HAVE A NICE WEEKEND, CHILDREN.

HAW HAW!

Y'KNOW, THAT *DOES* KINDA HURT.

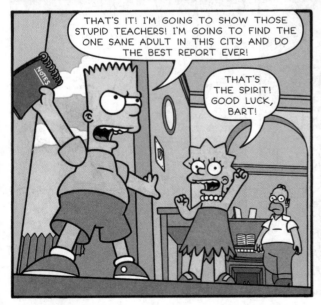

...AND THAT'S HOW I CONVINCED HER TO MARRY ME.

WITH BOTH EYES CLOSED?! THAT'S AMAZING.

BLAM! BLAM! BLAM!

ARE YOU SURE THESE EXPIRATION DATES DON'T JUST MEAN THE FOOD IS BAD TO EAT?

MANY TIMES THEY SIMPLY MEAN THAT THE OLD FOOD HAS BECOME A NEW PET.

...SO I SAID TO HER, "BESIDES THAT, MRS. LINCOLN, HOW DID YOU ENJOY THE PLAY?"

IT WAS AT THAT PRECISE MOMENT THAT XENA TOOK ME INTO HER ARMS AND BEGAN TO SMOTHER ME WITH HER HOT KISSES AND WARM CARESSES.

∶SIGH!∶ YOU REALIZE THAT THIS IS A *NONFICTION* ASSIGNMENT, DON'T YOU?

LOOK, MR. MOLEMAN, I CAN'T FIND ANYONE TO INTERVIEW FOR MY REPORT. I TRIED EVERYBODY. YOU'RE THE *LAST CHANCE* I'VE GOT.

HMMM. I'LL ONLY DO IT IF YOU TELL THEM *EXACTLY* WHAT I TELL YOU.

MISTER, YOU'VE GOT YOURSELF A DEAL.

WELL, IT ALL BEGAN LAST WEEK WHEN I ACCIDENTALLY FELL DOWN INTO THE CENTER OF THE EARTH.

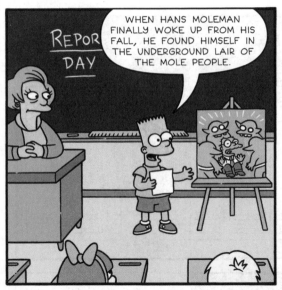

REPORT DAY

WHEN HANS MOLEMAN FINALLY WOKE UP FROM HIS FALL, HE FOUND HIMSELF IN THE UNDERGROUND LAIR OF THE MOLE PEOPLE.

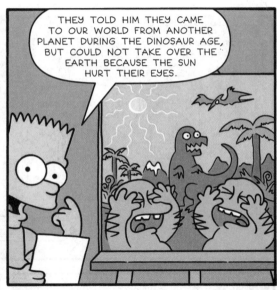

THEY TOLD HIM THEY CAME TO OUR WORLD FROM ANOTHER PLANET DURING THE DINOSAUR AGE, BUT COULD NOT TAKE OVER THE EARTH BECAUSE THE SUN HURT THEIR EYES.

THEY DECIDED TO LIVE UNDERGROUND WHERE THEY WERE ABLE TO SEE. IN TIME THEY BUILT A MASSIVE CITY AND INVENTED CURES FOR ALL THE SICKNESS AND DISEASE ON THE SURFACE. THIS WOULD BE THEIR GIFT TO US.

BUT THE MOLE PEOPLE WERE VERY SHY. WHEN HANS PROMISED TO GET THEM ALL SUNGLASSES, THEY DECIDED TO LET HIM LEAD THEM UP TO MEET US WHEN THE TIME WAS RIGHT.

THIS IS THE SECRET STORY OF HANS MOLEMAN, THE FUNNY LITTLE MAN THAT NOBODY CARES ABOUT. THAT CONCLUDES MY REPORT. ANY QUESTIONS?

OH, REALLY? DO YOU HAVE ANY *PROOF* THESE PEOPLE EXIST?

YES! I HAVE ASKED THEM TO MEET US HERE TODAY AT HIGH NOON. LADIES AND GENTLEMEN, IF YOU'LL LOOK OUT INTO THE HALLWAY TO MY LEFT...

BEHOLD! THE KING OF THE MOLE PEOPLE.

≩AHEM.≩

PERHAPS YOU CAN DO A *REAL* REPORT ABOUT THE ONE PERSON NOBODY INTERVIEWED...*PRINCIPAL SKINNER!*

COME ALONG, SIMPSON. IT LOOKS LIKE YOU'LL BE SPENDING A LOT OF TIME WITH ME THIS WEEK.

HA HA HA HA HA HA HA

VERY FUNNY, BART. THE NEXT THING YOU'LL BE TELLING ME IS THAT THEY STOPPED TO GET SOME COFFEE AND JELLY DONUTS ON THE WAY.

BUT HANS MOLEMAN SAID THEY'D BE HERE! HE REALLY DID!

SLAM!

I DON'T BELIEVE IT! MY WATCH STOPPED AT 11:30. ACCORDING TO THAT CLOCK, WE MISSED OUR CHANCE TO INTRODUCE YOU TO THE CHILDREN.

DINER

MMM...TOO BAD. WELL, I HAVE TO GET BACK TO THE EARTH'S CORE, OR I'LL BE LATE FOR THE SIGNING OF THE *MAGMA CARTA.*

≩GROAN!≩

THE END

I TELL YOU, EDNA...THE *WAITING* IS ALWAYS THE *WORST* PART!

I HEAR YOU, SEYMOUR!

MATT GROENING

EVERY DAY, I PRAY IT WILL BE DIFFERENT...BUT IT *NEVER* IS! NEVER IS NEVER IS NEVER IS...

GET A *GRIP*, SEYMOUR! WE CAN'T AFFORD TO SHOW *WEAKNESS!*

:AHEM!: Y-YOU'RE *RIGHT*, OF COURSE! A MOMENTARY *LAPSE*...

GET IT TOGETHER, MISTER! HERE THEY *COME!*

MODEL CITIZEN SIMPSON

EEEEEEKK!

NYAAH!

GOOD MORNING, PRINCIPAL SKINNER! GOOD MORNING, MRS. KRABAPPEL!

UHHHH... WHAT WAS *THAT*?!

I-I'M NOT SURE! IT WAS PLEASANT, SMILING, AND *POLITE*...

AFTER YOU, LADIES!

...AND YET IT *LOOKED* LIKE BART SIMPSON!

HE MUST BE *UP* TO SOMETHING!

WHAT *IS* HIS SCHEME?!

OH, THIS IS JUST *DISGUSTING*!

EXCUSE ME, GROUNDSKEEPER WILLIE, SIR. I BELIEVE YOU DROPPED THIS...?

ACH! *AWAY* WITH YE, LAD! I'LL NOT BE FALLIN' FOR ANY OF YOUR *DEMON* TRICKS--

OOOF!

WHUMP!

LISA! WHAT IS YOUR BROTHER *UP* TO?

:SIGH:: WHAT'S HE DONE *NOW*?!

THUMP! THUMP! THUMP!

HE'S BEING... *POLITE*!

UH-OH! THIS *CAN'T* BE GOOD!

LATER...

ALL MORNING IT'S BEEN *QUIET*... *TOO* QUIET!! BART'S BEHAVIOR HAS BEEN *PERFECT*...

...SO EITHER HE'S BEEN REPLACED BY A *CLONE*...OR THIS IS JUST THE *CALM* BEFORE THE STORM!

¡GASP!¿ H-HE'S *HERE*!

EXCUSE ME, LUNCHLADY DORIS, MAY I HAVE SOME...

YEEEEK!

BEFORE YOU SAY A SINGLE WORD, YOUNG MAN, YOU MARCH STRAIGHT UPSTAIRS...

...AND DO YOUR HOMEWORK! DON'T EVEN *THINK* ABOUT PLAYING BEFORE...

OF COURSE, MOM! HOMEWORK *BEFORE* PLAY! I'LL ALSO CLEAN MY ROOM BEFORE I GO!

HOMER! I THINK SOMETHING'S WRONG WITH BART!!

SOMETHING WORTH INTERRUPTING "ARE YOU SMARTER THAN A TV PRODUCER" FOR?!

I AM MOST SORRY, PRINCIPAL SKINNER, BUT I MUST CUT YOU OFF NOW...

...NOT BECAUSE YOU ARE ALL HOPPED UP ON CHERRY SQUISHEES, BUT BECAUSE YOU HAVE MAXED OUT YOUR DEBIT CARD!

I UNDERSTAND, APU! A PERFECTLY RATIONAL BUSINESS DECISION.

ANYWAY, THE SUGAR BUZZ HAS MADE ME FORGET THE CAUSE OF MY MISERY!

AND, APPARENTLY, MY *ADDRESS* AS WELL!

AH, SWEET SUGAR... THE EXCRUCIATING PAIN IN MY LEFT EYEBALL IS **WORTH** THE JITTERY FORGETFULNESS!

MOTHER WILL BE GETTING WORRIED! I'D BETTER HURRY HOME...

HMM! NOW **WHERE** DO I LIVE AGAIN...?

PARDON US, PRINCIPAL SKINNER!

HAVE A GOOD EVENING, SIR!

YIPES! NOW I REMEMBER!!

LOOK OUT, YA IDIOT!

MOTHER!

SKREEEEECH!

SPRINGFIELD **OIL**

FAWHOOM!

FWOOOOSSH!

NATE'S HOUSE OF FIREWORKS & DISCOUNT NITRATE FILM STOCK

SCREEEEEEECHHH!

THAWHOOOM!

WHAT THE HECK WAS THAT?!

BEATS ME... BUT *WHATEVER* IT IS, NOBODY CAN BLAME ME!

THE DAY BART SIMPSON *DIDN'T* MAKE TROUBLE... IT'S *HISTORIC!*

HEH! I TOLD YOU I COULD GO A WHOLE DAY ON MY *BEST* BEHAVIOR!

TOMORROW IT'S BACK TO BUSINESS AS USUAL, AND SPRINGFIELD... *BEWARE!*

WELL, I'LL BET EVERYBODY ENJOYED IT WHILE IT LASTED!

THE END

BART SIMPSON

in

AN EASY ASSIGNMENT

SERGIO ARAGONES
SCRIPT & ART

NATHAN HAMILL
COLORS

KAREN BATES
LETTERS

BILL MORRISON
EDITOR

FIRST THING WE NEED TO DO IS TO FIND A MAP AND LOOK FOR CUBE.

DO YOU MEAN *CUBA*?

NO. MRS. KRABAPPEL DEFINITELY SAID "*CUBE*."

ANYBODY WHO KNOWS *GEOMETRY* KNOWS WHERE CUBE IS!

OH BOY.

NO, *GEOGRAPHY* IS THE STUDY OF THE EARTH, ITS ATMOSPHERE AND POPULATION. AND THE COUNTRY ISN'T "CUBE," IT'S *CUBA*!

GEOMETRY IS THE BRANCH OF MATHEMATICS THAT STUDIES LINES, SOLIDS, AND SHAPES. YOU'LL HAVE TO BRING A *CUBE*.

LD ELEMENTARY SCHOOL

OH MAN, THE LITTLE DUDE IS CONFUSED. MAYBE I CAN GIVE HIM A HAND. IN SCHOOL, I WAS GOOD AT CHOREOGRAPHY.

MAYBE MAKING A CUBE WON'T BE THAT COMPLICATED!

AS SOON AS I FINISH, I'LL COME GIVE YOU A HAND. I'M GOOD AT LITHOGRAPHY!

OH BOY, IF OTTO HELPS, BART'S GOOSE IS COOKED!

SIMPSONS FLANDERS

FIRST, TO GET WHAT I NEED TO HELP BART WITH HIS TOPOGRAPHY. THIS PLACE HAS ALWAYS FULFILLED ALL MY NEEDS!

HEAD SHOP

HEY MAN, GIVE ME EVERYTHING I NEED TO BUILD A CUBE FOR A FRIEND.

GROOVY. I HAVEN'T BUILT ME A CUBE SINCE WOODSTOCK!

ZIG-ZAG

A CUBE. A CUBE. WHAT ON EARTH IS A CUBE?

I'M GOING TO THE BASEMENT TO USE YOUR TOOLS TO BUILD A CUBE FOR MY MATH CLASS. AND I DON'T EVEN KNOW WHERE TO START!

A CUBE... MATH...HMM?

I KNOW WHO TO ASK! LISA'S FRIEND. HE KNOWS SOMETHING ABOUT MATH!

HELLO, STEPHEN HAWKING? HI, GUY. I'M LISA SIMPSON'S FATHER, AND I NEED YOUR HELP. DO YOU KNOW WHAT A CUBE IS?

HI, PROFESSOR FRINK. I'M GOING TO BART'S TO BUILD A CUBE!

YUGA-HOY? A CUBE? LET ME GO TO MY CAR FOR SOME THINGS!

I HAVE SOME IDEAS FOR A CUBE TO END ALL CUBES.

DING DONG!

I HEAR YOU, MAN. I KNEW MY UNDERSTANDING OF PODIATRY WOULD COME IN HANDY!

ARE YOU TALKING ABOUT THE SYMMETRICAL THREE-DIMENSIONAL SHAPE, OR THE PRODUCT OF A NUMBER MULTIPLIED BY ITS SQUARE?

...BLACK HOLES COULD RADIATE IN TERMS OF QUANTUM MECHANICS. THEN A CUBE CAN BE SAID TO HAVE AN EQUAL...

DING DONG!

WHAT YOU SAID! SOMEBODY'S AT THE DOOR!

CLICK

¡VIVA LA BART!

BORING! LET'S SEE WHAT ELSE IS ON.

¡QUE LASTIMA!

PETER KUPER
SCRIPT & ART

EDWIN VASQUEZ
COLORS

KAREN BATES
LETTERS

BILL MORRISON
EDITOR

...AND IF THE PERSON WE CALL CAN ANSWER CORRECTLY, THEY'LL WIN AN ALL-EXPENSE-PAID TRIP FOR TWO TO MEXICO!

WHAT WAS THE NAME OF THE 1998-2006 SHOW BROADCAST ON MEXICO'S TV AZTECA NETWORK?

WE'VE PICKED ONE NAME AT RANDOM...

BOR--

RING!

CLIK

FEELING HOT? WHY NOT POP... AN ICE-COLD DUFF?

MR. SIMPSON, DO YOU KNOW THE ANSWER TO OUR QUESTION?

AYE, CARUMBA!

¡AY CARAMBA! IS CORRECT!

MATT GROENING

SHORTLY...

WHAT ARE WE WAITING FOR?

SURF'S ⦂GRUNT!⦂ UP, HOMBRE!

WHACK!

LAST ONE IN ⦂GRUNT!⦂ IS A ROTTEN ENCHILADA!

CHOP!

CHOP!

⦂GRUNT!⦂

WHACK!

WHACK!

CHOP!

⦂GRUNT!⦂

HEY, I THINK I SEE THE OCEAN THER--

OOOH!

LOOK, FELLAS, I THINK THIS IS A CASE OF MISTAKEN IDENTITY...

THE PREDICTIONS WERE TRUE! OUR ANCIENT HIGH PRIEST, QUETZALCOATORAMA, HAS RETURNED TO TAKE HIS RIGHTFUL PLACE!

YES, IT SEEMS TO BE TRUE..

BUT THERE IS ONLY ONE WAY TO BE SURE!

THE REAL QUETZALCOATORAMA WILL NOT BLEED!

YAAAAA!

WAIT...LOOK! ALL LOOK TO SEE A TOTAL ECLIPSE OF THE SUN.

PUT AWAY YOUR KNIFE. IT IS THE FINAL SIGN!

BUT-BUT...OH, FIDDLE-STICKS.

ALL HAIL QUETZALCOATORAMA!!

LOOK, THERE REALLY HAS BEEN SOME MIX-UP... I'M NOT WHAT'S-HIS-NAME.

PLEASE ACCEPT THESE SMALL GIFTS AS A TOKEN TO HONOR YOUR RETURN...

THIS IGUANA FOOT NECKLACE TO GIVE YOU COURAGE...

COOL!

THIS JAGUAR SKULLCAP SO YOUR BRAIN WILL BE WISE...

THE SUM OF THE SQUARE ROOTS OF ANY TWO SIDES OF AN ISOSCELES TRIANGLE IS EQUAL TO THE SQUARE ROOT OF THE REMAINING SIDE. *SWEET!*

THIS BAG OF SACRIFICED HUMAN HEARTS TO FORTIFY YOUR SOUL...

COURAGE? BRAINS? HEARTS?

LOOK, I LOVE *THE WIZARD OF OZ*, BUT I REALLY HAVE TO BE GOING.

AND LASTLY...

...THE SERVANT GIRL, FRIDA, WILL BRING YOU ALL THE CACAO YOU CAN EAT.

CACAO? WHAT'S THAT?

I BELIEVE YOUR PEOPLE CALL IT... *CHOCOLATE.*

CHOC--? *MMMM!*

QUETZALCOATORAMA IS IN THE HOUSE!

3 DAYS AND 4 NIGHTS LATER...

MORE, YOUR ROYAL HIGHNESS?

OHHH...I'M GOOD. *WELL*...MAYBE ONE MORE.

COME YOUR {AHEM} LORDSHIP, IT IS TIME FOR YOUR WORK.

WORK?!

YES, YOU MUST PERFORM THE RITUAL CLEANSING OF THE NEW PRISONER'S SOUL.

WHAT? I'VE GOT TO WASH SOME SMELLY--

YOU PERFORM THE CLEANSING BY REMOVING HIS HEART WITH THIS.

WHA--?! WHO IS THIS PRISONER?

HE IS SOME FORM OF MAN-APE WE FOUND IN THE JUNGLE.

HOMER?

WHY, YOU LITTLE--!

I'VE BEEN LOOKING FOR YOU SINCE THE ALL-YOU-CAN-EAT BUFFET RAN OUT!!

ACK!

BOW BEFORE QUETZALCOATORAMA!

YEAH, BOW BEFORE QUETZA--

ME!

Finito

GOOD MORROW, BRAVE READER! WELCOME TO THE EXCITING WORLD OF THE *VIKINGS AND VAMPIRES* ROLE-PLAYING GAME! I'LL BE YOUR GUIDE TO THIS FANTASY WONDERLAND. YOU CAN CALL ME...

GAMEMASTER LISA

...YOU REACH THE OUTSKIRTS OF THE FOREST KINGDOM OF MENSA.

"STIRRING"? THAT SOUNDS *DANGEROUS!* I'M DRINKING MY POTION OF HEALING!

DON'T WASTE THE POTION, DINGUS! OR YOU'RE GONNA NEED IT FOR *REAL* WOUNDS!

IT'S JUST A ROLE-PLAYING GAME, DOLPH. PERHAPS A SONG FROM THE ELVEN MINSTREL WILL CALM EVERYONE.

THE SUN IS SETTING. NIGHTFALL WILL BE UPON YOU SOON, AND THE CREATURES OF THE WOOD WILL BE STIRRING.

I'M *NOSE* PLAYING!

MATT GROENING

HEY, QUEEN OF THE DORKS, MOM SAID YOU HAVE TO PUT DOWN YOUR MAGIC SWORD AND HELP ME FOLD HOMER'S UNDERWEAR.

BART! WE'RE IN THE MIDDLE OF MY BIWEEKLY *VIKINGS AND VAMPIRES* ROLE-PLAYING GAME! YOU'RE RUINING THE ATMOSPHERE OF FANTASY!

WHOA! *DOLPH* PLAYS VIKINGS AND VAMPIRES? I THOUGHT THIS WAS STRICTLY A *NERD-FEST!*

UH-HUH... WELL, UH...

TONY DIGEROLAMO
SCRIPT

NINA MATSUMOTO
PENCILS

MIKE ROTE
INKS

NATHAN HAMILL
COLORS

KAREN BATES
LETTERS

BILL MORRISON
EDITOR

IF YOU EVER WANT TO EAT SOLID FOOD AGAIN, YOU'LL KEEP YOUR TACO HOLE SHUT, SIMPSON!

﹛GULP!﹜ YES, SIR.

DON'T LET HIM FOOL YOU, DOLPH. BART KEEPS A SECRET ABOUT AS WELL AS HE DOES LONG DIVISION IN HIS HEAD.

ARE YOU STILL ANGRY ABOUT THE TIME I SENT YOUR DIARY EXCERPTS TO THE SCHOOL PAPER? THAT'S ANCIENT HISTORY. GET OVER IT, LIS.

YOU DID IT YESTERDAY!

ALL RIGHT, SIMPSON, SINCE YOU DON'T KNOW HOW TO KEEP YOUR MOUTH SHUT...

...YOU'RE GONNA PLAY VIKINGS & VAMPIRES WITH US!

HUH?! ME? BUT DOLPH, WOULDN'T YOU RATHER HAVE SOMEONE WITH MORE DWEEBLIKE QUALITIES?

YOU'LL RISE TO THE CHALLENGE.

SEVERAL MINUTES LATER...

...AND FINALLY, WRITE DOWN YOUR DIGNITY SCORE. IF YOU LOSE TOO MANY POINTS YOUR CHARACTER BECOMES INDIGNANT.

GEEZ, LISA, HOMEWORK IS LESS HOMEWORK THAN THIS GAME!

HURRY UP AND FINISH. WE'VE GOT MONSTERS TO SLAY.

BACKGROUND MUSIC FROM "THE LORD OF THE RINGS."

CLICK

ALL RIGHT. RETURNING TO THE KINGDOM OF MENSA, OUR BRAVE HEROES...

"... MILHOUSE THE GRAY..."

I-I-I DON'T LIKE THE LOOKS OF THAT TREE.

"...WIZARD DOLPH OF WEERLON..."

GIMME YOUR GOLD OR EAT LIGHTNING, DINGUS!

"...EL RALPH THE KNIGHT..."

LIGHT-DING MAKES MY HAIR SCARED.

"...THEIR NEWEST MEMBER...;SIGH;... BOOGER MCBUTT THE CLERIC..."

MAN, THIS BITES.

"...MINSTREL MARTINA..."

♪ WITH MY LUTE I SING APOLLO'S MELODY! I LIVE WITH THE ELVES AND THEY NEVER JUDGE ME! WITH A HEY-NONNIE-NONNIE AND ♪ A HI-DI-HO-HEE! ♪

KA-ZAP!

...HAVE CREATED A FELLOWSHIP TO BATTLE EVIL IN THE DARK FORESTS.

BOORING! LET'S JUST GET IN THE CAR AND GO FIND A DRAGON.

GRRRR!

"YOU REACH THE MOUNTAIN AT THE EDGE OF THE KINGDOM. FAR IN THE DISTANCE, AT THE HIGHEST PEAK, SITS THE DARK, FOREBODING CASTLE AZURE. AT THE FOOT OF THE MOUNTAIN IS A SMALL ENVIRONMENTALLY FRIENDLY HUT."

IT TAKES FOREVER TO GET AROUND IN THIS STUPID GAME! I STILL SAY I SHOULD BE ABLE TO BUILD A ROCKET PACK.

"A BEAUTIFUL DRUID EMERGES FROM THE HUT."

I AM DRUID LISA, PROTECTOR OF THE FOREST. I KNOW NOT OF YOUR "ROCKET PACK," BUT AN EVIL VAMPIRE LIVES IN CASTLE AZURE AT THE TOP OF THIS MOUNTAIN.

TO SLAY HER AND HER MINIONS, YOU WILL NEED THESE MAGIC ITEMS. IT WILL BE A PERILOUS JOURNEY, FRAUGHT WITH EVIL!

WHY WOULD WE WANT TO KILL A COOL, BLOOD-DRINKING VAMPIRE? SHE'S NOT BOTHERING US.

DON'T YOU GET IT, SIR DORK-A-LOT? IF WE SLAY THE VAMPIRE AND HER MINIONS, SHE'S BOUND TO HAVE TREASURE AND COOL MAGIC ITEMS.

YEAH, BUT...

HOLY WATER

...IF DRUID LISA'S GIVING AWAY MAGIC ITEMS, *SHE* MUST HAVE A TON OF TREASURE AS WELL!

UH-OH.

HEY, YEAH!

GOOD CALL, MCBUTT. NOW WE HAVE TWICE AS MANY MAGIC ITEMS TO FIGHT THE VAMPIRE!

Y'KNOW, I THINK I COULD GET TO LIKE THIS GAME.

I DON'T THINK IT'S RIGHT THAT WE ROBBED DRUID LISA. THE ELVES HAVE A SONG ABOUT DISHONESTY...

SHOVE!

WAAAAAAAHHHH!

I'LL BET IF WE COME BACK LATER AFTER THE WOLVES ARE DONE EATING MARTINA'S CARCASS, WE CAN RECOVER THE LUTE *AND* SELL IT FOR GOLD.

HEY, GOOD CALL! YOU'RE A *NATURAL* AT THIS!

THUD!

LATER, INSIDE CASTLE AZURE...

OW! LI'L HELP?

I'M *SLAYING!*

FOOLS!

SMASHY-SMASHY!

NO ONE LEAVES CASTLE AZURE ALIVE! I AM *VAMPIREDNA*, AND FOR FIVE CENTURIES I HAVE RULED THESE LANDS. YOU FOOLS HAVE STUMBLED YOUR WAY INTO MY LAIR AND SLAYED MANY OF MY MINIONS. BUT THAT WAS ALL PART OF MY SECRET PLAN! FOR, YOU SEE--

AHHH! A WOODEN STAKE! BUT I WASN'T FINISHED WITH MY MONOLOGUE...

BART! THAT VAMPIRE WAS THE KEY TO THE WHOLE ADVENTURE! SHE WAS SUPPOSED TO TAUNT YOU FOR WEEKS AND YOU KILLED HER IN TWO MINUTES!

OH PLEASE! VAMPIRES *ALWAYS* TRY TO KILL YOU AFTER AN EVIL MONOLOGUE.

SWEET SLAYING, SIMPSON. YOUR BOOGER MCBUTT CHARACTER ROCKS!

KIDS! TIME TO WRAP UP YOUR GAME!

WITH ALL THE TREASURE POINTS WE GAINED, I SHOULD MAKE SIXTH LEVEL THIEF! THANKS, BART!

BART, PERHAPS YOU COULD PLAY NEXT WEEK TO HELP MY NEW CHARACTER CATCH UP TO THE REST OF THE GROUP.

NO PROBLEMO.

GRRRR! WITH BART'S NATURAL PROPENSITY FOR MAYHEM, HE COULD END UP *DESTROYING* MY WHOLE CAMPAIGN!

I BREATHED A DICE.

THE NEXT WEEK...

WELCOME, ADVENTURERS, TO THE HAUNTED MANOR OF PRESTO-BALSA! ONE HUNDRED AND SIXTY-SEVEN ROOMS OF SOUL-CRUSHING TERROR! HA, HA, HA, HA!

THE SECRETS OF THE MANOR AND ITS TREASURE LIE INSIDE ITS *GILDED HALLS*, GUARDED BY *TRAPS* AND *EVIL GHOSTS*!

EVIL GHOSTS, EH? *HOW* EVIL?

LET'S FIND OUT.

GILDED HALLS?! I'M *OUTTA* HERE!

WAIT A SECOND, CHUMS! I HAVE ONLY BEGUN MY QUEST AS MARTINA II!

WAAAAAAH!

I'M HELPING!

TOSS!

CRASH!

IT'S ALL CLEAR, CHUMS. COME ON IN!

≋WHEW!≋ *THAT'S* A RELIEF.

NOT SO FAST. WHY SHOULD WE EVEN BOTHER FIGHTING THESE EVIL GHOSTS...

...WHEN WE COULD JUST FIGHT THE HOUSE!

I SAW THIS IN A MCBAIN MOVIE WHERE HE'S A FIREMAN.

WAIT! WHAT ARE YOU DOING?

MY MANOR HOUSE! *AURRRGGH!*

FOOSH!

ONE MASSIVE FIRE LATER...

I FOUND A MELTED SILVER GOBLET!

I GOT SOME MORE MELTED COINS!

KEEP DIGGING, BOYS. WE STILL HAVE TO FIND MARTINA II'S LUTE.

BART...

THE NAME IS BOOGER. TRY AND STAY IN CHARACTER, LIS.

GRRR! BUT YOU'RE *RUINING* THE GAME! I SPENT *WEEKS* DETAILING THAT MANOR HOUSE, AND YOU BURNED IT DOWN IN AN HOUR!

YEAH, GOOD THING THERE WERE ONLY GHOSTS IN THERE. THAT PLACE WAS A *DEATH TRAP!*

THAT'S IT! I'VE GOT TO FIGURE OUT A WAY TO GET BART-- ER, *BOOGER*, OUT OF MY GAME!

THE NEXT WEEK...

WHO'S THE KING?

BOOGER! BOOGER! BOOGER!

THE WEEK AFTER...

BOYS, PICK UP MY TREASURE, WILL YOU? I'LL BE BACK AT MY CASTLE.

I THOUGHT THAT WAS *OUR* CASTLE.

WHATEVER, JUST MAKE WITH THE GOLD.

THE WEEK AFTER THAT...

REMEMBER, GUYS, JUST KEEP HITTING THEM WITH SILVER. I SAW IT IN *"WEREWOLF A GO-GO,"* A CLASSIC!

WAIT. WHERE ARE YOU GOING?

ARE YOU KIDDING? WITH ALL THE BOOTY WE MADE THIS MONTH, I WAS ABLE TO TAKE OVER THE KINGDOM. I'VE GOT A CORONATION TO PREPARE FOR! JUST MAKE SURE YOU GET THE TREASURE BACK TO MY PLACE.

THIS BITES! SINCE WHEN DO **WE** WORK FOR **HIM**?

HE'S RUINING THE GAME AND TAKING ALL THE TREASURE!

HEE-HEE! KITTY!

IF BOOGER BECOMES KING, THERE'LL BE NO STOPPING HIM.

I KNOW A WAY WE CAN GET BART TO QUIT THE GAME ON HIS OWN.

FELLOWS! LI'L HELP HERE! OW! FELLOWS?

THE WEEK AFTER THAT...

I HEREBY CROWN THEE KING BOOGER MCBUTT OF THE KINGDOM OF MENSA.

ALL RIGHT! FINALLY, SOME FANTASY RESPECT.

NOW THAT I'M KING, LET'S HAVE SOME FUN. WHAT HAVE WE GOT? TREASURE TO COUNT? FEASTS TO HOST? NOW I CAN FINALLY AFFORD TO BUY A BASEBALL TEAM, RIGHT?

ACTUALLY, YOUR HIGHNESS, YOU'LL NEED TO ISSUE SOME ROYAL DECREES TO KEEP THE KINGDOM RUNNING.

THE SEWERS NEED REPAIR ON THE EAST SIDE OF THE KINGDOM.

THE TANNERS' GUILD WANTS A REPEAL OF THE LEATHER TAX!

THE MINSTRELS ARE PROTESTING THE LUTE TAX!

I'M A PIRATE!

THE NEXT SEVERAL WEEKS...

THE ROYAL GUARD NEEDS NEW PANTS!

THE CITY NEEDS A NEW MOAT!

THE PEASANTS ARE DEMANDING HEALTH BENEFITS!

THE PARCHMENT ORDINANCE YOU SIGNED MEANS ALL THE DECREES NEED TO BE REWRITTEN!

THIS BITES.

I'M *OUTTA* HERE! THIS GAME'S BECOME LAMER THAN MOM'S VERSION OF MONOPOLY, WHERE WE HAD TO GIVE HER TWO HUGS WHEN WE PASSED "GO"!

IT LOOKS LIKE KING BOOGER MCBUTT HAS ABDICATED THE THRONE.

NOW THAT BART'S GONE, THE GAME CAN GET BACK TO NORMAL.

YEAH, BUT WE STILL NEED A CLERIC.

NEXT WEEK, I'LL HAVE A *NEW* PLAYER WHO CAN BE YOUR CLERIC...

"...AND SHE CAN'T POSSIBLY GET OUT OF CONTROL."

SHE'S *UNSTOPPABLE!* THIS IS *WORSE* THAN BART! WHAT DO WE DO?!

JUST KEEP RUNNING, DINGUS!

SUCK! SUCK!

THOOM! CRASH! CRUSH!

≡SIGH.≡ I WONDER IF IT'S TOO LATE IN THE YEAR TO JOIN THE CHESS CLUB.

THE END

MAGGIE'S CRIB

by ARAGONÉS

SERGIO ARAGONÉS
STORY & ART

NATHAN HAMILL
COLORS

BILL MORRISON
EDITOR

MONSTER MASHED

BELIEVE IT OR NOT, THAT ENDS ANOTHER QUEST IN SEARCH OF THE UNSOLVED MYSTERIES OF THE UNKNOWN ON *"MONSTER SAFARI!"*

THE COOLEST EPISODE YET!

YEAH! THAT WAS EVEN BETTER THAN THE STINK APE AND THE BURPING ANGEL.

MATT GROENING

"MONSTER SAFARI" IS ALWAYS LOOKING FOR CREATURES FOR OUR FEATURES! SEND PHOTOS, VIDEOS, AND EVIDENCE TO OUR STUDIOS, AND *YOU* COULD BE ON THE SHOW.

BE ON THE SHOW!?

JAMES W. BATES
SCRIPT

JAMES LLOYD
PENCILS

ANDREW PEPOY
INKS

ART VILLANUEVA
COLORS

KAREN BATES
LETTERS

BILL MORRISON
EDITOR

MILHOUSE, ARE *YOU* THINKING WHAT *I'M* THINKING?

SMOOCH!

MILHOUSE!

I SAID, ARE *YOU* THINKING WHAT *I'M* THINKING?

HUH?

WE NEED TO CATCH A MONSTER!

WHERE ARE WE GONNA FIND A MONSTER IN SPRINGFIELD?

I DUNNO, BUT THERE ARE HIDEOUS CREATURES EVERYWHERE.

ON "MONSTER SAFARI" THE FIRST THING THEY DO IS RESEARCH. WE HAVE TO HEAD TO THE LIBRARY.

OH.

WHAT'S WITH THE GET UP?

LET'S JUST SAY I HAVE A FEW LIBRARY BOOKS THAT I HAVEN'T RETURNED...

SPRINGFIELD PUBLIC LIBRARY

EXCUSE ME, WHERE DO YOU KEEP YOUR BOOKS ON CRYPTOZOOLOGY?

WANTED

FOR EXCESSIVE OVERDUE BOOK FEES

MAKE A RIGHT AT LITERARY CLASSICS, PASS WORLD HISTORY, TAKE A LEFT AT SCIENCE, AND YOU'LL FIND WHAT YOU'RE LOOKING FOR.

LET'S HIT THE BOOKS!

A MASTER'S DEGREE IN LIBRARY SCIENCE, AND ALL I DO IS TELL KIDS WHERE TO FIND BOOKS ABOUT THE LOCH NESS MONSTER.

WE'RE SURE TO FIND SOMETHING IN ONE OF THESE BOOKS!

WE'LL BE MONSTER HUNTING IN NO TIME!

THE JERSEY DEVIL

THIRTY MINUTES LATER...

OH NO! I'VE GONE BLIND!

NO YOU HAVEN'T. YOU JUST PASSED OUT WITH YOUR FACE IN A BOOK.

I GIVE UP. READING IS HARD.

MAYBE THE LIBRARY ISN'T THE ANSWER.

THERE ARE NO CREEPY CRAWLIES IN SPRINGFIELD.

I DON'T EVEN CARE ANYMORE ABOUT CATCHING ONE. I JUST WANT TO BE ON "MONSTER SAFARI."

THIS IS SO UNFAIR. IT WOULD'VE BEEN NICE TO BE FAMOUS.

WHY CAN'T STUPID SPRINGFIELD HAVE A STUPID MONSTER?

YOU'RE RIGHT. WHY *CAN'T* STUPID SPRINGFIELD HAVE A STUPID MONSTER?

THAT'S WHAT I *SAID!*

SO, IF WE CAN'T HUNT DOWN A CREATURE... WHY DON'T WE *MAKE ONE UP?* C'MON, WE KNOW HALF THE STUFF ON THAT SHOW IS FAKE.

HALF THE STUFF ON "MONSTER SAFARI" IS *FAKE?!*

I JUST FOUND OUR MONSTER.

YOU REALLY THINK WE CAN PASS OFF YOUR DOG AS A BEAST.

USE YOUR IMAGINATION! WITH A LITTLE COSTUMING AND A DASH OF SHOWMANSHIP, SANTA'S LITTLE HELPER WILL CAUSE NIGHTMARES ACROSS THE COUNTRY.

LICK! LICK! LICK!

GOOD BOY! THE CHUPACABRA IS A DIRTY CREATURE!

DID I MENTION THE DRY CLEANING BILL?

YOUR DOG'S NOT VERY SMART, BART. ARE YOU SURE WE CAN PULL THIS OFF?

SURE! WATCH THIS!

STAND UP, BOY!

SPEAK!

ARF! ARF! ARF!

OKAY. WHAT ABOUT THE HORNS?

LET ME GET OUT THE SUPPLIES.

ZIP!

I DUMPSTER-DOVE FOR SOME T-BONES AT GREASY JOE'S BOTTOMLESS BARBECUE PIT.

WE'RE GONNA TAPE THEM TO THE DOG'S HEAD?

BRILLIANT, ISN'T IT?

GREASY JOE'S

HERE, BOY!

THIS IS KENT BROCKMAN REPORTING FROM THE SPRINGFIELD RETIREMENT CASTLE WHERE SOME OF THE GERIATRIC RESIDENTS CLAIM TO HAVE SPOTTED A MONSTER!

CAN YOU GENTLEMEN REALLY BE SURE OF WHAT YOU SAW?

AS SURE AS LYNDON JOHNSON IS PRESIDENT OF THE UNITED STATES!

I SAW IT CLEAR AS DAY, AND I'VE GOT 20/200 VISION!

LET'S GET OUT OF HERE.

I THINK WE CAN CHALK THIS UP TO EXTRA MEDS IN THEIR JELL-O.

WAIT! WE HAVE PROOF!

HMM...IT'S INTERESTING.

BUT PRETTY BLURRY.

WELL, I'M NOT A PRO LIKE YOU.

I THINK WE *DO* HAVE A STORY. YOU BOYS WANT TO BE INTERVIEWED?

THOUGHT YOU'D NEVER ASK!

TOLD YOU!

HOW DOES MY HAIR LOOK?

BOYS, TELL US YOUR AMAZING STORY.

WELL, KENT, WE'VE BEEN ON THE TRAIL OF THIS CHUPACABRA FOR A WHILE NOW.

YOU COULD SAY WE'VE BEEN ON A *MONSTER SAFARI*.

LIKE THE POPULAR TV SHOW?

OH. NOW THAT YOU MENTION IT, I GUESS THERE *IS* A TV SHOW WITH THAT NAME.

I GOT A 9-1-1 CALL ABOUT A MONSTER? WHAT GIVES?

YOU SHOULD ASK THIS ADEPT DUO OF MONSTER HUNTERS!

WE SAW THE LEGENDARY CHUPACABRA.

GREAT GOOGLY MOOGLY! WE'D BETTER FIND AND KILL THAT THING!

GRRR!

THE END

MILHOUSE VAN HOUTEN PRESENTS
A GUY'S GUIDE TO GOING OUT WITH GALS

UNLUCKY IN LOVE?
WELL, IF YOU'RE LIKE ME,
YOU BLAME YOURSELF, BUT LET'S FACE IT,
GIRLS SEND OUT MORE MIXED SIGNALS THAN
A SEMAPHORE FLAG WAVER WITH HEAD LICE. THAT'S
WHY I'M OFFERING UP THESE SURE-FIRE TIPS
FOR NAVIGATING THE TEMPESTUOUS
SEA OF LOVE.

DATING DON'Ts & DOs

DON'T

· Be yourself. Imagine the kind of guy that a girl would go on a second date with and then pretend to be that guy.

· Relax and have a good time. This will only lead to you doing or saying or being something stupid.

· Have anything to eat or drink. Food is messy and liquids make you squirmy.

· Be considerate. Chicks love bad boys. At least that's what I read in Cosmo.

· Be too picky. Remember, if a girl accepts a date with you, her standards aren't very high either.

· Let her out of your sight for a minute. She's liable to make a break for it and run home.

· Call her the next day. She may have already forgotten who you are. Call her the minute you get home from your date.

DO

Everything on the "don't" list.

MATT GROENING

ASK MILHOUSE

Q: Are there some things men are simply expected to do for women?
M: Oh, boy! Are there ever! Whoa! I'll say! Don't get me started! Oh, man!

Q: What are some of these things?
M: I have no idea.

Q: What is the proper way for a boy to ask a girl for a date?
M: Please? Please? *Pleeeeeeeeeeeeease?*

THE PATENTED VAN HOUTEN DATE ASKER DE-HUMILIATOR

IN MY COPIOUS SPARE TIME, I HAVE DEVELOPED A TECHNIQUE FOR ASKING FOR A DATE THAT HAS THE YOUNG LADY'S REFUSAL BUILT RIGHT INTO THE PROPOSAL. THIS WAY, A GIRL CAN'T TURN ME DOWN WITHOUT SAYING "YES"!

DO YOU WANT TO GO THE MOVIES WITH ME ON SATURDAY, OR DO YOU HAVE TO WASH THE CAT?

YES, I DO

CAN I WALK YOU HOME, OR DO YOU PREFER TO USE PUBLIC TRANSPORTATION AND SPEND 40 MINUTES SITTING IN THE HOT SUN ON A FILTHY BENCH WAITING FOR THE CROSSTOWN BUS?

OH, YES. ANYTIME.

WILL YOU LET ME CALL ON YOU TOMORROW NIGHT, OR WILL YOU BE HAVING YOUR APPENDIX REMOVED *AGAIN*?

YES, I WILL.

MAY I TAKE YOU TO THE SPRING DANCE NEXT WEEK, OR WOULD YOU JUST AS SOON STAY HOME ALL ALONE AND GO STARK RAVING MAD STARING AT THE WALLPAPER?

GOSH, YES. THAT'S SOUNDS *GREAT!*

HOW ABOUT LUNCH SOME AFTERNOON, OR WOULD YOU RATHER DIE AND ROT IN HELL FIRST?

YES, WE WOULD! THANK YOU VERY MUCH. SOUNDS GREAT!

MAGGIE'S CRIB

by ARAGONÉS

SERGIO ARAGONÉS
STORY & ART

NATHAN HAMILL
COLORS

BILL MORRISON
EDITOR

GREETINGS, SALUTATIONS, AND THE HELLO-HOW-ARE-YOUS-WITH-THE-CURIOSITY-AND-THE-CONCERN! I AM HERE TODAY ON BEHALF OF THE *ENVIRONMENTAL PROTECTION AGENCY* TO SERVE YOU WITH AN INJUNCTION.

OH MY! WHAT ARE YOU INJUNCTING *US* ABOUT?

THE WAY YOU *LIVE!* WE HAVE DETERMINED THAT YOUR HOUSEHOLD'S LIFESTYLE HAS CREATED A HOLE IN THE *OZONE LAYER* ABOVE YOUR DOMICILE, WHICH ⌐NG-HEY!⌐ WOULD EXPLAIN WHY YOUR HAIR IS ON FIRE.

MARGE GOES GREEN!

GREAT SAGAN'S GHOST! YOUR HAIR IS ON FIRE!

AHHHH!

MATT GROENING

SCOTT M. GIMPLE
SCRIPT

MIKE KAZALEH
PENCILS & INKS

ART VILLANUEVA
COLORS

KAREN BATES
LETTERS

BILL MORRISON
EDITOR

MRS. SIMPSON, YOUR FAMILY HAS TO CHANGE ITS WAYS BEFORE YOUR HOME IS DESTROYED BY UV RADIATION, CARBON EMISSIONS, AND THE VAST AMOUNTS OF *METHANE* PRODUCED BY YOUR HUSBAND! ⸭GA-HOYVEN!⸭

P-SSHT!

OH REALLY? WELL, IT'S EASY TO POINT FINGERS. WHAT, MAY I ASK, ARE *YOU* DOING TO HELP?

IN ORDER TO PREVENT AN ECOLOGICAL APOCALYPSE OF *WATER-WORLDIAN* PROPORTIONS, I HAVE DECIDED TO DRASTICALLY REDUCE MY WASTEFUL OUTPUT.

I AM NOW SOLELY REPRESENTED BY AN INCORPOREAL HOLOGRAM, ELIMINATING MY CARBON FOOTPRINT...AS WELL AS MY *ACTUAL* FOOTPRINT.

HOWEVER, IT'S AN EXPERIMENT THAT HAS GONE HORRIBLY, *HORRIBLY* AWRY.

SFFZZT!

HRMMM...I DON'T WANT TO GET ON THE EPA'S BAD SIDE AGAIN.* I SUPPOSE I *COULD* BE A BIT MORE DEDICATED TO THIS "GOING GREEN" THING...

*EDITOR'S NOTE: AS CHRONICLED IN THE NOW-CLASSIC FILM, "THE SIMPSONS MOVIE" - BILL

AND SOON...

MOM, WHAT'S IN YOUR HAIR?

THEY'RE POTATOES! BY BAKING THEM AND USING THEM AS CURLERS BEFORE DINNER, I'M KILLING TWO ENERGY BIRDS WITH SEVERAL POTATOES!

IT'S FOR RECYCLING MY EMPTY DUFF CANS?

AND IT'S *MADE* FROM DUFF CANS, TOO!

UGH! WHAT IS THAT NOISE?

BLAH BLAH BLAH BLAH BLAH BLAH

NO MORE TOXIC BUG SPRAY OR POISONOUS RAT POISON FOR THE SIMPSON FAMILY. TO KEEP PESTS AWAY, WE'LL JUST USE *CHELSEA HANDLER'S* PODCAST!

UH, HOMER, I THINK MOM'S LOSING IT.

I DON'T KNOW...IT SAYS HERE THESE BRIQUETTES ARE MADE FROM PEACH PITS, PETRIFIED OREOS, AND OOOOH!...STALE PUMPERNICKEL HEELS!

Mesquite Marge's HOME MADE CHARCOALESQUE BRIQUETTES

FAMILY, WE NO LONGER HAVE TO WASTE PRECIOUS WATER IN THE SHOWER WITH ALL THE TIME IT TAKES TO SOAP UP! BEHOLD, BUCKETS OF PRE-LATHERED LATHER!

I BET THE KIDS AT SCHOOL WOULD KILL TO HAVE A SHIRT MADE FROM LAWN CLIPPINGS!

I BET THE KIDS AT SCHOOL WILL KILL THE PERSON WEARING THIS SHIRT. AT THE VERY LEAST, I THINK DOGS WILL PEE ON HIM.

MARGE, IT'S ALMOST THREE IN THE MORNING... WHY ARE THE WALLS ALIVE WITH LIGHT?

BECAUSE I PAINTED THEM WITH GLOW-IN-THE-DARK LATEX! IT PROVIDES ALL THE RADIANT LIGHT OF A LAMP WITHOUT USING ANY ELECTRICAL POWER WHATSOEVER!

UM. CAN YOU TURN IT OFF?

LOOK, MAGGIE! WE'RE WATERING THE HOUSEPLANTS, COOLING THE DINING ROOM, AND PROVIDING YOU WITH HIGH QUALITY TODDLER-TAINMENT WHILE DRYING YOUR FATHER'S UNMENTIONABLES AT THE SAME TIME!

EXCITING NEWS, FAMILY! I'VE ARRANGED TO HAVE MYSELF COMPOSTED WHEN I DIE!

THE NEXT DAY...

MOM, I COMMEND YOU ON YOUR DEDICATION TO LIVING MORE ECO-FRIENDLY...BUT MAYBE YOU'VE GONE A BIT TOO FAR.

MAYBE YOU CAN FOCUS ON THE LITTLE THINGS THAT HELP THE ENVIRONMENT...LIKE USING COFFEE GROUNDS AS MULCH INSTEAD OF THROWING THEM IN THE GARBAGE.

HMMM...MAYBE I *HAVE* GONE A TAD OVERBOARD. IN MY QUEST TO LEAVE A SMALLER CARBON FOOTPRINT, I MAY HAVE STEPPED ON SANITY'S TOES.

WHAT DO YOU SAY WE TAKE A TAKE A NONPOLLUTING WALK FOR AN ORGANIC TREAT?

THEY HAVE CAROB SQUISHEES AT THE KWIK-E-MART...?

SUSTAINABLY SOLD!

IS IT FINALLY OVER?

I THINK SO, BOY. WE CAN PLUG THE REFRIGERATOR BACK IN AND STOP WEAVING OUR OWN TOILET PAPER FROM OLD NEWSPAPERS.

GOOD GRIEF. MOM ONLY STARTED THIS CRUSADE *YESTERDAY*.

YOU HEAR THAT, BOY? WE WENT GREEN FOR A WHOLE DAY! NOBODY CAN ASK MORE OF US THAN THAT!

HRMM...

THE END

BART SIMPSON: WARLORD

CHRIS YAMBAR
SCRIPT

SCOTT SHAW!
PENCILS & INKS

NATHAN HAMILL
COLORS

KAREN BATES
LETTERS

BILL MORRISON
EDITOR

HEAR ME WELL, SIMPSON. YOU WILL ADDRESS ME WITH THE DIGNITY THAT MY STATURE DEMANDS, OR YOU WILL BE *EXPELLED* FROM THE PREMISES AND MISS THE OPPORTUNITY TO MEET...

RADIOACTIVE MAN!

HELLO, CHILDREN. I AM HERE TO SAVE THE DAY BY SIGNING YOUR COLLECTIBLES.

OOOH! OOOH! ME FIRST! I'M YOUR *BIGGEST FAN!*

IN MORE WAYS THAN ONE!

THERE'S NO WAY I'M WAITING IN THAT LINE.

I'LL HIDE BEHIND THIS GIANT GORILLA SO NO ONE CAN SEE ME TRANSFORM FROM MILD-MANNERED BART SIMPSON...

...INTO SPRINGFIELD'S GREATEST RESIDENT SUPERHERO!

IT IS TIME TO DISCUSS YOUR MISSION. COME WITH US NOW OR BE BANISHED INTO DEEP SPACE WHERE YOUR EVERY MOLECULE WILL EXPAND AND EXPLODE LIKE A BLOB OF GOO IN A COSMIC MICROWAVE.

WE MADE SOME LEMONADE.

LEMONADE? BRING IT ON!

TELL US, HOW DID THESE VILLAINS COME TO POSSESS YOUR SPACESHIP?

THE MARTIANS ARE THE BIGGEST BULLIES IN THE GALAXY. THEY HAVE ALWAYS BEEN AFTER OUR SPACESHIP.

HMMM. ¡SLURP!¡ BULLIES...

IS RADIOACTIVE MAN ALL RIGHT? HE CAUSED US SOME CONCERN WHEN HE RAN OFF LIKE THAT.

OH, UMM...YEAH! HE WAS JUST LOOKING FOR A CONTACT LENS THAT POPPED OUT. HE'S STILL GETTING USED TO WEARING THEM INSTEAD OF HIS READING GLASSES.

A SUPERHERO WHO SECRETLY WEARS GLASSES?! IS THERE NO END TO THE MYSTERIES OF THIS PROFESSION?

AFTER THEY STOLE OUR SHIP, THEY STRANDED US HERE. WE USED OUR LAST BIT OF RESERVE ENERGY TO TRANSPORT YOU HERE TO HELP US.

HMMM. HELP YOU. I SEE.

THAT STILL DOESN'T EXPLAIN WHY THEY WANTED YOUR SPACESHIP IN THE FIRST PLACE.

WELL...WE... UM...

OH, ALL RIGHT.

THEY GOT US. YOU MIGHT AS WELL TELL THEM THE WHOLE STORY, KANG.

"WE HAD JUST RECEIVED A TOP SECRET MISSION FROM THE INTERGALACTIC COUNCIL."

"WE WERE TO TRANSPORT A DANGEROUS BLACK HOLE TO THE OTHER SIDE OF THE UNIVERSE BEFORE IT EXPANDED AND WIPED OUT ALL LIFE IN OUR SECTOR."

"WE WERE WELL ON OUR JOURNEY THROUGH THE MILKY WAY WHEN WE WERE SPOTTED BY THE MARTIAN MONGOLS."

"WE WERE CAPTURED AND BROUGHT TO MARS. NOW THE MARTIANS HAVE THE BLACK HOLE AND OUR SPACESHIP."

WE NARROWLY ESCAPED THEIR GRASP. IF THEY OPEN THAT CONTAINER, WE'RE ALL DOOMED!

WHY DIDN'T YOU CONTACT THE INTERGALACTIC COUNCIL?

THEY WOULD HAVE FIRED US AND MADE FUN OF US BEHIND OUR BACKS.

WORRY NO LONGER. POINT US IN THE DIRECTION OF YOUR SHIP AND WE WILL DROP THE HAMMER OF JUSTICE UPON YOUR FOUL AND FIENDISH FOES!

I'VE GOT A PLAN. AND ALL YOU HAVE TO DO IS *ACT*!

I CAN DO THAT.

JUST DO EXACTLY AS I SAY.

WE'LL WEDGE ONE END OF THIS PLANK BETWEEN SOME OF THESE HEAVY DRUMS AND MAKE A DIVING BOARD.

YOU'LL SPRING OFF THE BOARD AND LAND ON THOSE MATTRESSES DOWN THERE. THEY'LL THINK YOU FLEW IN AND THAT YOU'RE A *REAL* SUPERHERO.

THEN YOU'LL ANNOUNCE THAT YOU'RE *RADIOACTIVE MAN* AND THAT YOU'VE COME FOR THE SPACESHIP.

WHILE YOU HAVE THEIR ATTENTION, I'LL USE MY SLINGSHOT TO KNOCK ONE OF THEIR BURNING TORCHES INTO THAT PILE OF FUEL BARRELS. WITH ANY LUCK IT'LL EXPLODE AND MAKE THEM THINK THAT *YOU* DID IT WITH YOUR ATOMO-VISION.

THEY'LL BE SO STUNNED, THEY'LL SURRENDER WITHOUT A FIGHT. THE ART OF *ILLUSION* IS ALL WE'VE GOT. WE WON'T GET A SECOND CHANCE.

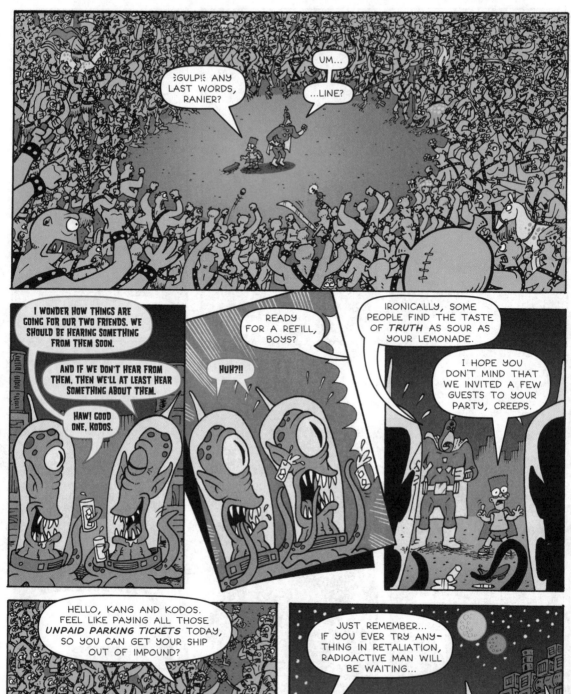

:GULP!: ANY LAST WORDS, RANIER?

UM...

...LINE?

I WONDER HOW THINGS ARE GOING FOR OUR TWO FRIENDS. WE SHOULD BE HEARING SOMETHING FROM THEM SOON.

AND IF WE DON'T HEAR FROM THEM, THEN WE'LL AT LEAST HEAR SOMETHING ABOUT THEM.

HAW! GOOD ONE, KODOS.

READY FOR A REFILL, BOYS?

HUH?!!

IRONICALLY, SOME PEOPLE FIND THE TASTE OF *TRUTH* AS SOUR AS YOUR LEMONADE.

I HOPE YOU DON'T MIND THAT WE INVITED A FEW GUESTS TO YOUR PARTY, CREEPS.

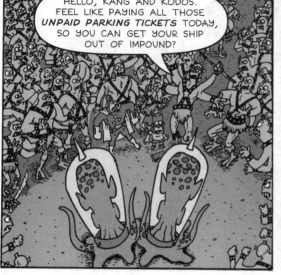

HELLO, KANG AND KODOS. FEEL LIKE PAYING ALL THOSE *UNPAID PARKING TICKETS* TODAY, SO YOU CAN GET YOUR SHIP OUT OF IMPOUND?

JUST REMEMBER... IF YOU EVER TRY ANYTHING IN RETALIATION, RADIOACTIVE MAN WILL BE WAITING...

...WAITING TO EAT YOU BOTH LIKE THE *CALAMARI* YOU SO DELICIOUSLY RESEMBLE.

TAKE US AWAY!

HURRY BEFORE HE BECOMES HUNGRY!

WE HAD TO SEIZE THEIR VEHICLE IN ORDER TO GET THEM TO PAY THEIR 423,783 UNPAID PARKING TICKETS.

WOW! I CAN'T IMAGINE OWING ANYONE THAT MUCH MONEY. THAT'S JUST CRAZY!

OBVIOUSLY YOU'VE NEVER HAD TO PAY A PERCENTAGE TO A HOLLYWOOD AGENT!

WE'RE SORRY THAT YOU GOT ROUGHED UP BACK THERE. THANKS FOR HELPING US CATCH THOSE SCOFFLAWS.

SLAP!

JUST DOING OUR JOB, MAN. GLAD TO HELP.

ONE MORE THING. CAN I HAVE YOUR AUTOGRAPH? WE DON'T GET A LOT OF SUPERHEROES OUT HERE.

NO PROBLEMO!

IT WOULD BE GREAT IF YOUR *SIDEKICK* COULD SIGN THIS FOR ME, TOO.

⫶SNORT!⫶

NOW IF YOU'LL KINDLY STEP INTO OUR MATTER TRANSPORTER, WE'LL WHISK YOU BACK TO EARTH WHERE YOU'LL REAPPEAR THE EXACT SECOND THAT YOU WERE ABDUCTED. NO ONE WILL EVEN KNOW THAT YOU WERE GONE.

IN TIME, EVEN YOU WILL FORGET ABOUT THIS EVENT AND COME TO THINK OF IT AS A HARMLESS DAYDREAM.

HEY, WOLFCASTLE. WERE YOU SERIOUS ABOUT *EATING* THOSE ALIENS BACK THERE? I MEAN, THAT *WAS* KIND OF GROSS.

HA! I WAS MESSING WITH THEIR MINDS. I'M HIGHLY ALLERGIC TO SEAFOOD. I WAS SIMPLY *ACTING!*

NICE! I THINK YOU HAVE THE POTENTIAL TO BECOME A *REAL* SUPERHERO. YOU KNOW, LIKE *ME!*

NO THANKS. I'M TOO DELICATE FOR THIS LINE OF WORK.

THE END.

MAGGIE'S CRIB

by ARAGONÉS

SERGIO ARAGONÉS
STORY & ART

NATHAN HAMILL
COLORS

BILL MORRISON
EDITOR

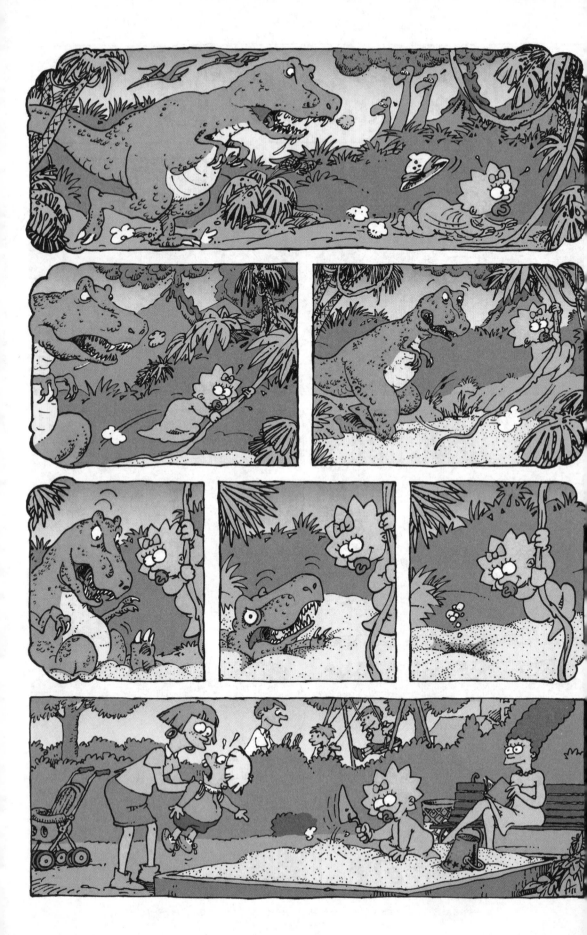

"I'M LISA SIMPSON, WHO THE HECK ARE YOU?"

TIME TO MAKE MY *COMEBACK!* NO ONE BEATS ME AT KRUSTY BOWL-A-RAMA!

UH, BART, DON'T YOU THINK YOU SHOULD PUT ON THE WRIST STRAP JUST TO BE SAFE?

C'MON, LIS, THAT'S JUST A *SUGGESTION*...

ZWOOT!

WHUH-OH!

TWHACK!

OW!

WHUMP

LISA?! OH NO!

C'MON, LISA! WAKE UP! *I'M* THE ONE WHO'S DESTINED TO DIE PLAYING VIDEO GAMES!

SHE'S STILL BREATHING... ≥PHEW!≤

I GUESS THE NEXT LOGICAL STEP IS...

MOM! DAD!

LATER, AT THE HOSPITAL...

...I *BEGGED* LISA TO USE THE STRAP ON HER CONTROLLER, BUT SHE WOULDN'T LISTEN! IT CAME FLYING OUT OF HER HAND AND HIT HER IN THE FACE!

I'VE DONE THAT WITH THE TV REMOTE SO MANY TIMES, I'VE *LOST COUNT*.

I DON'T KNOW...THAT JUST DOESN'T SOUND LIKE SOMETHING LISA WOULD DO.

MR. AND MRS. SIMPSON, LISA'S *AWAKE*.

BUT I'M AFRAID I HAVE SOME *BAD NEWS*...

...THE HOSPITAL CAFETERIA RAN OUT OF JELL-O.

DR. HIBBERT, WHAT ABOUT *LISA*? HOW IS *SHE* DOING?

WHY? *WHYYYY*?

AH HEE HEE HEE! RIGHT, RIGHT...LISA! SHE'S FINE...WELL, EXCEPT FOR ALL THE AMNESIA.

≥GASP!≤ *AMNESIA*?!

HONEY, IF WE HAVE JELL-O, THERE'S *NOTHING* WE CAN'T GET THROUGH.

A MOMENT LATER...

HI, SWEETIE! DO YOU REMEMBER WHO *I* AM?

UHHH...MY *NURSE?*

MR. AND MRS. SIMPSON, IT'S HARD TO SAY HOW LONG THIS WILL LAST.

THE BEST WAY TO HELP LISA REGAIN HER MEMORY IS BY CONSTANTLY REMINDING HER OF WHO SHE IS AND WHAT SHE LIKES TO DO.

IT'S ESPECIALLY IMPORTANT FOR *YOU* TO HELP, BART. ARE YOU UP FOR THE CHALLENGE?

I'LL DO EVERYTHING I CAN!

A FEW DAYS LATER...

SO BART, SINCE I CAN'T REMEMBER A *SINGLE THING* ABOUT WHO I AM...

...WHAT KIND OF KID AM I?

WELL... UH...YOU'RE THE GOO--

DON'T TELL HER *SHE'S* THE GOOD KID! MESS WITH HER A LITTLE AND TELL HER SHE'S *THE NAUGHTY ONE*...

...AND THAT *YOU'RE* THE ANGEL!

HEY, HOW COME I HAVE *TWO* DEVILS ON MY SHOULDERS?!

YOU *USED TO* HAVE AN ANGEL, BUT SINCE YOU ALWAYS *IGNORED* HIM, HE MOVED AWAY.

NOW TELL LISA HOW *EVIL* SHE REALLY IS!

WELL, YOU SEE...*YOU* ARE THE BAD KID, AND *I'M* THE GOOD ONE.

REALLY?

AS FAR AS YOU KNOW. FOR INSTANCE, EVERY MORNING WHEN WE GET ON THE BUS, YOU START A *SPIT-BALL FIGHT!*

THAT JUST DOESN'T *FEEL* LIKE SOMETHING I'D DO. BUT IF YOU SAY THAT'S THE WAY I AM...

IF I SAID IT, IT MUST BE *TRUE!*

NOW, IT'S VERY IMPORTANT FOR YOU TO DO THE STUFF YOU'RE USED TO IN ORDER GET YOUR MEMORY BACK!

HERE'S A STRAW. I'LL RIP UP THIS PIECE OF PAPER FOR YOUR *AMMUNITION!*

A MOMENT LATER...

TWHOOOT!

ATTAGIRL, LIS!

WHAT THE--?!

SPITBALL?!

SPITBALL FIGHT!

YAAAAAAAAY!

"WELL, I DON'T KNOW WHAT TO SAY, SIMPSON..."

THIS KIND OF BEHAVIOR IS...*UNEXPECTED*, TO SAY THE LEAST. BUT CONSIDERING YOUR RECENT ACCIDENT...

...I'LL LET YOUR INDISCRETION SLIDE THIS *ONE TIME,* PROVIDING YOU HELP OTTO CLEAN THE BUS DURING RECESS.

YOU'RE FREE TO GO TO CLASS, LISA...

...BUT IF I SEE YOU IN HERE AGAIN, DETENTION WILL BE THE *LEAST* OF YOUR WORRIES!

NO *DETENTION?! NO WAY!*

LOOKS LIKE I HAVE MY WORK CUT OUT FOR ME IF I'M GOING TO GET LISA INTO THE KIND OF TROUBLE *I'M* USED TO!

OVER THE NEXT FEW DAYS...

El Barto.

SPPPSSSSSS!

LISA S.

HELLO, I'M LOOKING FOR MRS. *BUTTOOKIS.* IVANA IS THE FIRST NAME...?

IVANA BUTTOOKIS! IVANA BUTTOOKIS, PLEASE! IS THERE A BUTTOOKIS *HERE*?!

THAT'S *HER!* THAT'S THE LITTLE GIRL THAT *DEFACED* ME!

LISA

LISA, BART...I HAVE TO ASK YOU A FEW QUESTIONS ABOUT SOME *SPRAY-PAINTING* ALLEGATIONS...

GET BENT, FAT MAN!

OWWWIE-OW-OW!

STOMP!

YOU'RE COMING TO THE STATION, MISSY!

LISA?! WHY DID YOU *DO THAT?!*

IT'S LIKE YOU SAID, BART. *I'M* "THE BAD ONE..."

...AND IT WAS AFTER I CONFRONTED HER ABOUT THE GRAFFITI AND LITTERING THAT SHE *ASSAULTED* ME!

I-I-I JUST CAN'T BELIEVE MY LITTLE LISA COULD *DO* THIS!

IT'S THE STRANGEST THING, MRS. SIMPSON... BUT IT'S ALMOST AS IF SHE'S *SWITCHED PERSONALITIES* WITH BART!

PRINCIPAL SKINNER, WHAT ARE YOU EVEN DOING HERE AT THE POLICE STATION?

TIMES ARE TOUGH, SO I TOOK A *SECOND JOB*...

I COME HERE AFTER SCHOOL TO MAKE EXTRA CASH *FINGERPRINTING* THE CRIMINALS!

LATER...

I JUST DON'T UNDERSTAND HOW LOSING HER MEMORY HAS ALSO TURNED LISA INTO A *TROUBLEMAKER*.

WHY DID YOU STEP ON CHIEF WIGGUM'S FOOT? I NEVER SAID THAT WAS SOMETHING YOU USED TO DO!

YOU DIDN'T HAVE TO. I JUST KNEW THAT WAS SOMETHING THE *OLD* LISA WOULD'VE DONE...

...AND I *LOVED* IT!

OH NO! I'VE CREATED A *MONSTER*! I HAVE TO GET THE REAL LISA BACK BEFORE IT'S *TOO LATE*!

A FEW MINUTES LATER...

GO STRAIGHT TO YOUR ROOM, LISA! YOU'RE *GROUNDED!*

CRUD, I HAVE TO ACT FAST!

HEY, LIS, HOW 'BOUT A QUICK GAME OF KRUSTY BOWLING IN MY ROOM BEFORE YOUR GROUNDING BEGINS?

SOUNDS GOOD TO ME!

THE OLD LISA WOULD DEFINITELY *DEFY* MOM AND DAD *ONE LAST TIME!*

A MOMENT LATER...

COME ON, BART, WE DON'T HAVE *ALL DAY!*

JUST MAKING SURE YOU'RE IN THE *RIGHT SPOT...*

EL BARTO   STRIKEGIRL

FOR *WHAT?!*

FOR *THIS!*

AGCK! TWHACK!

MAN, I HOPE THIS *WORKS...*

LATER, BACK AT THE DOCTOR'S OFFICE...

WELL, IT LOOKS LIKE LISA HAS A RARE CASE OF *RE-AMNESIA!* SHE'S FORGOTTEN THE THINGS SHE DIDN'T KNOW SHE ALREADY KNEW! AH HEE HEE HEE!

I TOLD HER NOT TO PLAY THAT GAME AGAIN, MOM! I FEEL LIKE THIS IS *ALL MY FAULT!*

OH, BART, YOU OF ALL PEOPLE KNOW THAT WHEN SOMEONE MAKES UP THEIR MIND TO MISBEHAVE THEY CAN'T BE *STOPPED!*

AS TRUE AS THAT MAY BE, I PROMISE YOU *THIS,* MOM AND DAD...

...I WON'T LEAVE LISA'S SIDE UNTIL SHE REMEMBERS THAT SHE'S A *PAIN-IN-MY-BUTT,* GOODY *TWO-SHOES* AGAIN!

THE FOLLOWING WEEK...

THE END

MAGGIE'S FIRST DAY

SERGIO ARAGONÉS
STORY & ART

ART VILLANUEVA
COLORS

BILL MORRISON
EDITOR

DANGER
FUSION
IMMINENT

SAFE
FUSION
AVERTED

ZZZ

WACK!

THE FACE THAT LAUNCHED A THOUSAND BLECCHS

ARIE KAPLAN
SCRIPT

PHIL ORTIZ
PENCILS

MIKE DECARLO
INKS

NATHAN HAMILL
COLORS

KAREN BATES
LETTERS

BILL MORRISON
EDITOR

SEVERAL FAILED ATTEMPTS LATER...

I DON'T UNDERSTAND IT! I JUST CAN'T SEEM TO SCARE HIM BACK TO NORMAL. IT'S REALLY WEARING ON MY SELF-CONFIDENCE.

I CAN ⸞UNGH!⸞ TELL. YOU REALLY DON'T ⸞OOF!⸞ SEEM LIKE YOURSELF.

OH, YEAH? THINK *YOU* COULD DO ANY BETTER, DINGUS?

HMM...MAYBE I CAN...

HEY, BART! I'VE GOT YOUR NOSE! SEE? IT'S HERE IN MY HAND. OOOH, SCARY...

WHAT IS MILHOUSE DOING?

SCARING ME SO THAT MY FACE UNFREEZES.

REALLY?

WELL, IN A WORLD OF PEOPLE AS GULLIBLE AS MILHOUSE, MAYBE. IN *THIS* REALITY, NOT SO MUCH.

⸞SIGH.⸞ I WISH SOMEONE *WAS* ABLE TO SCARE ME BACK TO NORMAL. MY FACE IS *REALLY* STARTING TO HURT FROM BEING STUCK LIKE THIS.

NOW I KNOW WHAT *JOAN RIVERS* FEELS LIKE.

I KNOW SOMETHING THAT SCARES YOU.

REALLY? WHAT?

SNAP!

THIS!

SMOK!

HEY, KNOCK IT OFF!

I DON'T GET IT! BEING HUGGED AND KISSED BY A GIRL SHOULD'VE SCARED YOU BACK TO NORMAL.

PFFT! *YOU'RE* NOT A GIRL.

YES, I AM.

NUH-UNH! SISTERS DON'T COUNT. IT'S NOT LIKE YOU'RE SHERRI OR TERRI OR JANEY OR JESSICA LOVEJOY OR GRETA WOLFCASTLE OR...

HMMM...

AND SO...

SMEK!

HEY! QUIT IT!

HEY!!

SMOK!

SMEK!

WOW, BART...

END